MY FIRST BOOK OF DINOSAURS

Illustrated by
Zoë Ingram

WALKER BOOKS
AND SUBSIDIARIES
LONDON • BOSTON • SYDNEY • AUCKLAND

Did you know?

Coelophysis had a wishbone, just like a modern-day chicken.

Dinosaur facts

Weight	27 kg
Diet	carnivore
Where	USA, South Africa and Zimbabwe
When	225–190 million years ago (mya)
Pronunciation	see-LOE-fie-sis

Coelophysis

Coelophysis was one of the earliest dinosaurs and looked a bit like a huge bird, with a long S-shaped neck. It was quick and agile, and had sharp teeth and claws that made it an excellent hunter. Like a bird, it had hollow bones, which meant it was very light.

Size

Height: 2 m

Length: 2 m

Diplodocus

This giant plant-eater had an incredibly long neck that it used to reach leaves on the highest branches. It grew very quickly, reaching full size in about ten years. Its name, which means “double beam”, comes from the two-pronged bones in its tail.

Size

Height: 8 m

Length: 27 m

Dinosaur facts

Weight	15,000 kg
Diet	herbivore
Where	North America
When	155–145 mya
Pronunciation	DIP-loe-DOE-kus

Did you know?

Its teeth wore down really quickly and new ones grew every 35 days.

Dinosaur facts	
Weight	3,100 kg
Diet	herbivore
Where	USA
When	155–145 mya
Pronunciation	steg-oe-SAW-rus

Did you know?

Stegosaurus had a very small brain – about the size of a satsuma!

Stegosaurus

Stegosaurus means "roofed lizard". Palaeontologists chose the name because they thought that its spiky plates lay flat along its back like tiles on a roof! Scientists still aren't sure what the purpose of the plates was. They may have helped cool Stegosaurus down or scared off predators like the spikes on its tail.

Size

Height: 4 m

Length: 9 m

Allosaurus

Allosaurus was a fierce predator. It had jaws that opened incredibly wide and were full of pointed teeth. Its strong, sharp claws could grow up to 20 cm long – twice the length of a tiger's! The most famous Allosaurus is "Big Al", a nearly complete skeleton that was found in Wyoming, USA.

Size

Height: 5 m
Length: 12 m

Did you know?
Allosaurus's teeth curved backwards to stop prey escaping.

Dinosaur facts

Weight	2,000 kg
Diet	carnivore
Where	USA and Portugal
When	155–144 mya
Pronunciation	AL-oe-saw-rus

Dinosaur facts

Weight	80,000 kg
Diet	herbivore
Where	USA, Portugal and Algeria
When	155–140 mya
Pronunciation	BRAK-ee-oe-saw-rus

Did you know?

Palaeontologists estimate that Brachiosaurus could have lived to 100 years of age.

Brachiosaurus

This giant vegetarian had a nine-metre-long neck that enabled it to reach food on very high branches. Each of the bones in its neck was one metre long! It would have needed a large, strong heart to pump blood all the way up to its brain. The name Brachiosaurus means "arm lizard", which comes from the fact that its forelegs were much longer than its hind legs.

Size

Height: 16 m

Length: 26–30 m

Apatosaurus

This giant was closely related to the Brontosaurus – in fact, at one point, scientists thought that they were the same dinosaur. It had strong thick legs to support its massive body, and its footprints would have been a metre wide!

Size

Height: 4.6 m
Length: 21 m

Did you know?

Apatosaurus eggs could measure up to 30 cm – that's the length of a rugby ball!

Dinosaur facts

Weight	20–30,000 kg
Diet	herbivore
Where	USA
When	154–145 mya
Pronunciation	a-PAT-oe-saw-rus

Did you know?

Despite looking just like a bird, Archaeopteryx probably couldn't fly very well!

Dinosaur facts

Weight	less than 1 kg
Diet	carnivore
Where	Germany
When	150 mya
Pronunciation	ark-ee-OP-ter-ix

Archaeopteryx

Archaeopteryx, which means "ancient wing", was a feathered dinosaur that had sharp, pointed teeth – and claws on its wings! When Archaeopteryx fossils were first discovered, they were thought to be birds, and they are still the closest known link between birds and dinosaurs. Archaeopteryx had a bony tail, unlike modern birds, whose tails are made of muscle and feathers.

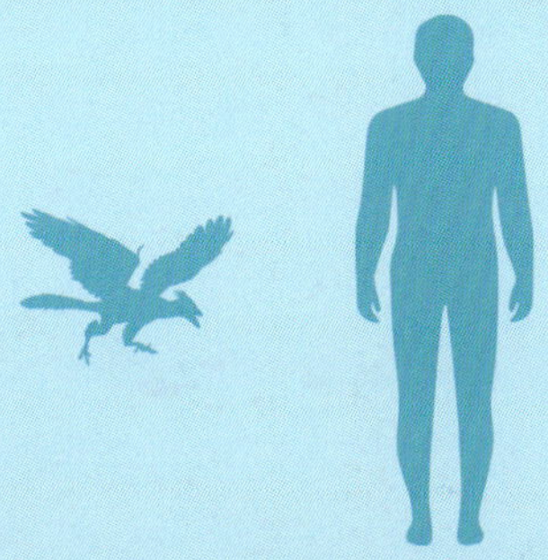

Size

Height: 0.3 m

Length: 0.5 m

Compsognathus

Compsognathus was the fastest of all the dinosaurs. With an estimated top speed of 64 kph, this small dinosaur walked on its back legs and could run 100 metres in less than six seconds. Although it was only the size of a chicken, Compsognathus was really fierce!

Size

Height: 0.7 m
Length: 0.65 m

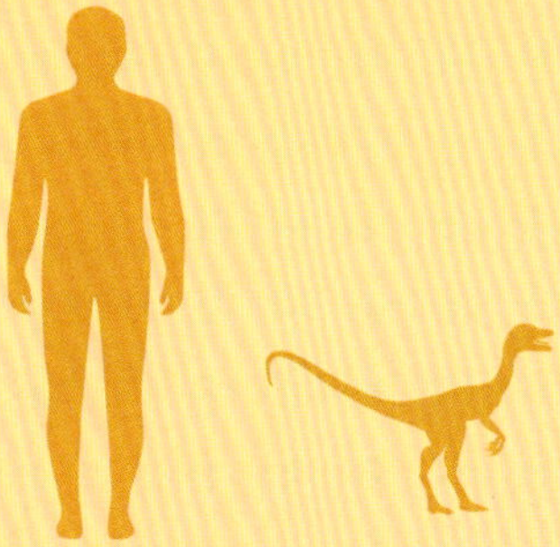

Dinosaur facts

Weight	3 kg
Diet	carnivore
Where	France and Germany
When	145–140 mya
Pronunciation	komp-sog-NAYTH-us

Did you know?
Compsognathus means "elegant jaw".

Did you know?

30 complete Iguanodon skeletons were uncovered in a mine in Belgium in 1878. What a discovery!

Dinosaur facts

Weight	4,000 kg
Diet	herbivore
Where	Belgium and UK
When	140–110 mya
Pronunciation	ig-WAH-noe-don

Iguanodon

Iguanodon was one of the largest herbivores. It could walk on two feet or four and had a tough beak for biting, with large teeth at the back of its mouth for chewing. Iguanodon was one of the very first dinosaurs to be discovered, in Sussex in 1822.

Size

Height: 5 m

Length: 10 m

Baryonyx

This dinosaur was only discovered in 1983, in the UK. It particularly liked to eat fish and had a long crocodile-like snout that prevented its wriggly prey escaping. The name Baryonyx means "heavy claw" and comes from the very large claw – probably on its thumb – that it would have used as a fishing hook.

Size

Height: 3 m

Length: 10 m

Did you know?

Baryonyx had almost twice as many teeth as Tyrannosaurus rex.

Dinosaur facts

Weight	2,000 kg
Diet	carnivore
Where	UK and Spain
When	125 mya
Pronunciation	bah-ree-ON-ix

Dinosaur facts

Weight	225 kg
Diet	herbivore
Where	Australia
When	121–112 mya
Pronunciation	MIN-mee

Did you know?

Minmi was about the same weight as a medium-sized modern-day pig!

Minmi

Minmi was a small armoured dinosaur that walked on four legs. It moved slowly and grazed on grasses and vegetation. Its skin was covered with bony plates and spikes that would have helped protect it from predators.

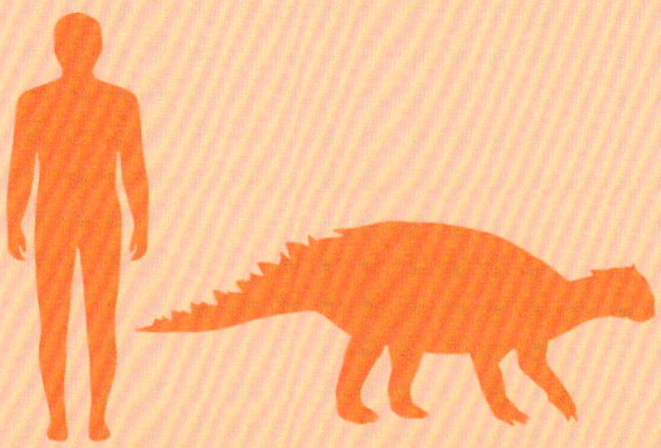

Size

Height: 1 m

Length: 2–3 m

Giganotosaurus

This huge dinosaur, whose name means "giant southern lizard", was even bigger than Tyrannosaurus rex! It weighed less, though, which meant it could run faster, and for long distances. It had a very small brain in relation to its size.

Size

Height: 6 m

Length: up to 16 m

Did you know?

Giganotosaurus was only discovered in 1993, by an Argentinian called Rubén Carolini.

Dinosaur facts

Weight	8,000 kg
Diet	carnivore
Where	South America
When	112–90 mya
Pronunciation	ji-gan-OE-toe-saw-rus

Dinosaur facts

Weight	4,000 kg
Diet	carnivore
Where	Egypt and Morocco
When	95–70 mya
Pronunciation	SPY-noe-saw-rus

Did you know?
Only six Spinosaurus skeletons have ever been found and they were incomplete. There is a lot more still to be learned about this dinosaur!

Spinosaurus

Spinosaurus was probably the largest of the carnivores – even bigger than Giganotosaurus! The enormous sail on its back was held up by spines that were 1.5 metres long and was probably used to attract a mate, as well as to help it control its body temperature. It lived in and out of water and liked to eat fish.

Size

Height: 5–6 m

Length: 18 m

Oviraptor

Oviraptor was a bird-like dinosaur with a strong, toothless beak that it used to crush hard objects and crack open fruit and shellfish. It had a long, muscular tail, which would probably have been covered in feathers, and sharp claws to protect itself.

Size

Height: 0.8 m
Length: 2 m

Dinosaur facts

Weight	20 kg
Diet	omnivore
Where	Mongolia
When	85–75 mya
Pronunciation	OE-vee-rap-tor

Did you know?

Oviraptor means "egg thief" – although there is little evidence that it actually ate other dinosaurs' eggs.

Did you know?
The name Velociraptor means "rapid robber"!

Dinosaur facts

Weight	7–15 kg
Diet	carnivore
Where	Mongolia
When	74–70 mya
Pronunciation	vel-OS-ee-rap-tor

Velociraptor

This small bird-like dinosaur probably had a fine feathery covering. It was small but fast, and scientists think that it would have been able to run at speeds of up to 40 kph. A fierce hunter, it had very sharp teeth and claws.

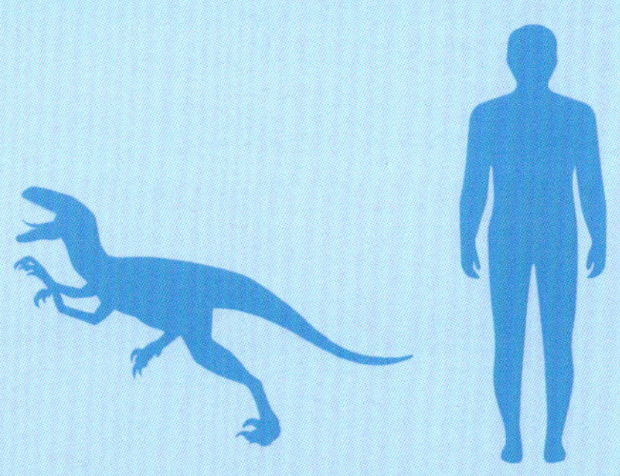

Size

Height: 1 m

Length: 2 m

Parasaurolophus

This duck-billed dinosaur lived in groups. It probably used the tubes in the crest on top of its head to communicate with other members of the herd – a bit like playing a trombone. It could walk on either two legs or four and run for short distances. Very few Parasaurolophus fossils have ever been found.

Size

Height: 4.6 m
Length: 11 m

Did you know?

Its huge head crest could grow up to 1.8 m long. That's longer than the height of an average human adult.

Dinosaur facts

Weight	3,500 kg
Diet	herbivore
Where	Canada and USA
When	76–74 mya
Pronunciation	pa-ra-saw-ROL-off-us

Dinosaur facts

Weight	200 kg
Diet	omnivore
Where	Mongolia
When	74–70 mya
Pronunciation	ga-lee-MEE-mus

Did you know?

Gallimimus's brain was the size of a golf ball.

Gallimimus

Gallimimus probably looked like a modern-day ostrich with fluffy feathers and – at over 60 kph – it could run really fast like an ostrich too. Its long tail would have helped it keep its balance as it ran. Scientists think that it may have used its beak to filter food from water, just like ducks do today.

Size

Height: 3 m
Length: 6 m

Troodon

Of all the dinosaurs, this small meat-eater had the largest brain in proportion to its overall size. But while it was the most intelligent of all the dinosaurs, it was probably only as clever as a modern-day chicken! It had large forward-facing eyes that meant it could see depth and track its prey more easily.

Size

Height: 0.9 m

Length: 2 m

Did you know?

Troodon had 122 teeth!

Dinosaur facts

Weight	40 kg
Diet	carnivore
Where	USA
When	74–65 mya
Pronunciation	TROE-oe-don

Dinosaur facts

Weight	5,500 kg
Diet	herbivore
Where	USA
When	68–66 mya
Pronunciation	try-SAIR-a-tops

Did you know?
Triceratops is the official state dinosaur of Wyoming, USA.

Triceratops

Triceratops is famous for its giant neck frill and the three horns that give it its name. It had the largest skull of any land animal. Triceratops lived at the same time as Tyrannosaurus rex and would have used its horns to help defend itself.

Size

Height: 3 m

Length: 9 m

Tyrannosaurus rex

Tyrannosaurus rex was the most terrifying of all the dinosaurs and could crunch through solid bone. With a large brain and binocular vision, T. rex was an awesome predator. It could run short distances at speeds of over 30 kph.

Size

Height: 5.6 m

Length: 12 m

Did you know?

T. rex had 50–60 teeth. Some were as long as a banana.

Dinosaur facts

Weight	up to 7,000 kg
Diet	carnivore
Where	Canada and USA
When	68–66 mya
Pronunciation	ty-RAN-oe-saw-rus REX

Index

○ **Iguanodon**

Page 20

○ **Minmi**

Page 24

○ **Oviraptor**

Page 30

○ **Parasaurolophus**

Page 34

○ **Stegosaurus**

Page 8

○ **Spinosaurus**

Page 28

○ **Triceratops**

Page 40

○ **Troodon**

Page 38

○ **Tyrannosaurus rex**

Page 42

○ **Velociraptor**

Page 32

For the roaringly awesome
"Dream Team", Nic and Jamie.
And Gracie-May and Max.

First published 2023 by Walker Books Ltd
87 Vauxhall Walk, London SE11 5HJ

2 4 6 8 10 9 7 5 3 1

Illustrations by Zoë Ingram

This book has been typeset in Futura,
Montserrat, Nevis and Aunt Mildred

Printed in China

British Library Cataloguing in Publication Data:
a catalogue record for this book is available
from the British Library

ISBN 978-1-5295-0997-7

www.walker.co.uk